Inuit Tales

UNIT 10

By Barbara Gunn

Adapted by Marilyn Sprick, Richard Dunn, and Shelley V. Jones

Illustrated by Susan Jerde

Main Characters

This is Tim

Who is this?

This is Grandpa.

Who is this?

This is Aunt Bea.

Who is this?

Vocabulary Words

Mukluks

Parka

Mittens

Table of Contents

Inuit Tales

DUET STORIES: Adults read the small text. Students read the large text.

Inuit Tales

CHAPTER 1 • MEET TIM

My name is Tim. My family and I are Inuit. We live in a fishing village in Northern Canada. The days and nights are very different where we live. In the summer, it's light all day, and most of the night too. But in the winter, it is dark most of the day and night!

Who is this story about? (Tim)

I'm Tim, and this is where I live.

I see the all day in the summer.

I see the at night too!

It would be very different to have the sun out all night.

1

Every day my father goes out fishing and my mother takes care of my baby sister, Josie. Grandpa sits in front of our house carving animals and birds out of stone. Once he even carved a little kayak for me.

What does Grandpa do? (Carve animals and birds)

Meet .

I see sit in front of the house and carve a

whale. It looks just like the whales that swim in the sea.

Every day I go to school with my older brothers, Sam and Matt. School is fun because we're learning to speak the Inuit language. At recess we play baseball.

Look at the picture. What are the children doing?

Sam and Matt are playing baseball on the school playground.

• • •

What game do Tim and his brothers like to play? (Baseball)

CHAPTER 2

Tim and

Meet .

Tim said, "I see sit in the ."

Who does Tim see? (Grandpa)

 sees Tim.

• • •

Tim and seem .

• • • • •

Look at the clothes that Tim and Grandpa are wearing. Do you think it's cold where they live?
How can you tell?

CHAPTER 3 • DOG TEAM TRIP

At night, after dinner, Grandpa tells us stories about when he was young. He tells us how his family traveled by dog team during the winter. He tells us how his family lived in igloos that they built out of blocks of ice.

That is a good storyteller.

We sit and listen to his stories about the old days.

Nod your head if you think Tim likes to hear Grandpa's stories.

Sometimes Grandpa still hitches the dog team to the sled. He takes my brothers with him to go fishing. Sometimes they visit old friends. I always ask Grandpa if I can go too, but he says I'm too young.

What does Tim want to do? (Go with his grandpa on a trip)

Tim says,

"I'm sad. Sam and Matt seem

• • • • • •

to be having fun helping Grandpa with the dog team."

Why was Tim sad? (He wanted to go with his Grandpa.)

It is Saturday morning. Sam and Matt go out fishing with Father. The house is quiet. Then Grandpa says, "Tim, I'm going to visit Aunt Bea. Would you like to come along?" I pull on my parka and mukluks, but I'm so excited I almost forget my mittens.

Why do you think Tim is excited? (He gets to go on a trip with Grandpa.)

Look at the picture on the next page. Tim put on his parka. A parka is a warm jacket. Touch Tim's parka. He also put on his Mukluks. What do you think mukluks are? Touch Tim's mukluks.

Grandpa says,

"Tim, I need your help.

Matt and Sam have gone fishing.

I need your help with the dogs."

Tim says,

"I'm .

I get to take a trip on the dogsled with Grandpa."

We hitch the dogs to the sled. I help Grandpa put booties on the dogs' feet to protect them from sticks and rocks on the trail. Grandpa yells "Mush!" and we take off across the snow. Grandpa talks to Tam, the lead dog of the team, telling him where to go and where to turn. Grandpa says,

"Tim, see that Tam.

•   •   •   •

Tam is a very smart dog."

•

Grandpa yells "Mush!" and we take off across the snow.

CHAPTER 4
Sweet Tam

 said, "Meet Tam the

sweet . See Tam sit.

I'm in the .

I see Tim in the ."

CHAPTER 5

Aunt Bea

Grandpa and I are going to Aunt Bea's. Grandpa lets me help guide the sled until my arms get tired; then he takes over.

See , and Tim, and the .

Tam is leading the team.

Tim is helping Grandpa guide the dogsled.

When we get to Aunt Bea's house, Grandpa steps on the sled brake and calls, "Whoa," to stop the dogs. We tie the dogs to a stake in the snow and give them food and water.

Aunt Bea gives Grandpa and me a hug. Then she makes tea while we take off our parkas and mukluks. Inuit children are taught to listen while the grownups are speaking. I play with Aunt Bea's cats as she and Grandpa catch up on the family news.

After the grownups talk, Aunt Bea says, "Tim, did you bring games to play?" I hadn't, so she gives me a bag of marbles to play with.

Grandpa and I can't stay long because the days are getting shorter. There are no lights or roads to guide us home. We hitch the dogs to the sled, hop on, and wave goodbye.

Why do Grandpa and Tim have to get home before dark?

See Tim sit in the dogsled.

Tim and seem like they are having fun.

On the ride home, I hear the "swoosh" of the sled runners skimming over the snow. I hear the dogs barking, and I hear Grandpa talking to the dogs.

"Tim, did you ever help me today!" says Grandpa.

"We make a good team — just like the dogs make a good team.

I am proud of you."

Why was Grandpa proud of Tim?

Do you think Tim will get to help with the dog team again?

 Tim

 was in the .

 said, "I need that Tim.

I need Tim and Tam."

Tim sat in the .

Tim was .

Who's the story about? (Tim)

Why was Tim happy? (He got to go in the sled with Grandpa.) 17

UNIT 1	UNIT 4	UNIT 6	UNIT 8	UNIT 10
*I	am	Dee	meet	did
I	Sam	mad	sat	in
		*the	seems	Matt
			Tamee	Tam
UNIT 2			that	Tim
see	**UNIT 5**			sees
2	Dad	**UNIT 7**		sit
	sad	an		*was
	*said	and	**UNIT 9**	
UNIT 3	3	man	at	
I'm		seem	Nan	
me			need	
			seeds	
			sweet	
			we	
			weeds	